THE FARING LIGHT LETTERS

A MAGICAL SORT OF MEMOIR

Ailene Cuthbertson

Leaping Blue Books

"The Faring Light Letters" is a work of creative nonfiction. While based on real life and true events, the author has taken sweeping creative liberties with names, characters, dates, places, events, details, physics, and pretty much everything. Because this is her story. And this is how she wants to tell it.

Copyright © 2023 by Ailene Cuthbertson

This book is copyright. Except for the purpose of fair review, no part may be stored or transmitted in any form or by any means, electronic or mechanical, including recording or storage in any information retrieval system, without permission in writing from the publishers. No reproduction may be made, whether by photocopying or by any other means, unless a licence has been obtained from the publisher or its agent.

ISBN 978-0-473-67707-7 (Paperback)

ISBN 978-0-473-67708-4 (Epub)

ISBN 978-0-473-67709-1 (Kindle)

ISBN 978-0-473-67710-7 (Apple Books)

Cover art and design by Ailene Cuthbertson

*For Jack and Isabella
and Kep*

Contents

To the Reader ... vii

1. Waikato, New Zealand — May 13th 2012 ... 1
2. Ring of Fire, A Border Realm — Oct. 30th 2012 ... 5
3. West Quarter, A Bohemian Realm — May 4th 2015 ... 13
4. An Island Off the Edge of the Map,
   An Undisclosed Realm — Jan. 16th 2016 ... 21
5. The Nest, An Island Realm — Feb. 14th 2018 ... 27
6. Waikato, New Zealand — May 8th 2022 ... 37

Acknowledgements ... 41
About the Author ... 43

To the Reader

I am glad some of these letters survive.

Several, I believe lost in the post. Others, I found floating in ink-stained water during the great bathtub flood of a year and a half ago. The final straw was the unfortunate number that were eaten to a pulp by a band of rogue, giggling snails. Therefore, in order to preserve these few that remain, I have had them copied and bound in the slim volume you hold in your hands.

And, while you may not be the intended recipient, now these letters are for you.

They're for you whenever you're feeling a bit off, lost, dissatisfied, stuck in the rat race, ho-hum, plain ol' *beige*.

Whenever you're finding yourself thinking, "Is this all there is?" or "I will be happy when…"

Whenever you're realising your life is composed of 'oughts' and you start to wonder who you really are.

Whenever you're trying to start anew after everything has been thrown topsy-turvy.

To the Reader

Whenever you're taking the next step to follow a new dream, or letting go of an old one.

And, most importantly, whenever you're asking yourself, "Where did the magic go?"

No matter where you are and what threshold you're crossing, I wish you the very best. May you find your magic. May you find your story. May you follow your inklings, your heart, and your dreams. May you jump boots and all into adventures, shouting "allons-y!" on a regular basis.

And may you find your own dryads, mermaids, and dragons all over the worlds.

Ailene

Chapter 1

Waikato, New Zealand
May 13th 2012

Dear Jack and Isabella,

I have been thinking of you more than ever today. Although, that's hardly surprising, given what day it is.

I'm not entirely sure why I'm writing. You find me without much to tell you, except, perhaps, I'm now in possession of two cupcakes.

Two obscenely cheerful cupcakes that turned my morning into a not-so-comic farce.

I'd better start at the beginning.

You wouldn't know the shop — it's cute, with a Victorian tea room sort of air. As usual, I still hadn't decided as I stepped up to the counter. The trio in front of me had made easy-to-guess choices — chocolate for mum, what looked like blueberry for the boy, and pink with sparkles for the girl. Shocker.

But, for myself? I had wandered in because I remembered what delightful pick-me-up treats they made. But now, as I stared at them — squatting in the cabinet, all dressed up in frosting — I wasn't so sure.

You can't blame me for feeling somewhat maudlin, deciding that perhaps I should choose one to match my mood. But then, what flavour is grief? Bitter, with a sour aftertaste? It would have to be black, of course. Black like the hole that had swallowed my future. And, to continue the metaphor, it would also need a vital ingredient missing. Or the heart torn out of it. Or contain peanut butter — which, I maintain, is enough to make anyone cry.

I barely registered the shop girl's, "Hello, how are you?" followed by a giggle. She sounded as sweet as the baking in the cabinet beside her. I admit to a fleeting, somewhat petty, thought of telling her. Fortunately for her, my brain supplied my mouth with a socially acceptable response.

Her next question presented me with a binary choice and an easy one at that. Eat here — alone, by myself, surrounded by the laughter of somewhat sticky families? I chose to take away.

I pointed randomly at an apple cinnamon crunch and a red velvet. With a, "Ooo, good choices, my favourites," and another giggle, the girl scooped the cupcakes into a paper box. She made it sound like any choice would've had the same claim to favouritism. I wondered what she might actually prefer — rainbows, sparkles, and unicorn sneezes — and was unprepared for her next question in our thus-far rote interaction.

"Do you have a loyalty card?" she asked as she poked a manicured, glitter-tipped finger at the till. Why yes, not only did I have a loyalty card, but I thought I may be due a free cupcake. That'd be nice.

She swiped the plastic and reeled off my name and phone number from her screen. At this point, I wish hindsight had given me a swift kick on the shin. Because,

Waikato, New Zealand – May 13th 2012

right here, was my first mistake. I asked her to change my last name. She curved her raspberry-red lips into a, "Congratulations!"

I could see why she'd jumped to that conclusion — the sparkler on her left hand and the rounded stomach pushing against her uniform apron. My brain provided another stock response. And, then (seriously, where was hindsight when I needed it) tacked on my second mistake: "You too."

She draped a possessive hand over her stomach.

"Just married," she beamed, "Didn't even want to start a family so soon but it just happened." The glittery fingers slid my loyalty card across the counter towards me and she added, "How about you? Kids?"

Given what day it was, I'd walked right into that one. And over the years, I've learned that evasions — such as an admission of fur babies — only elicited expressions of pity.

I told her I did not.

"Oh," she said. And then it came, dripping out of those smiling, bright red lips. "Oh, but you're young," she said, "Plenty of time."

The words slipped into my ears, through my guard, and smashed a straight punch to my solar plexus. Its sibling, "But of course you want kids?" is more of a feint and jab but the result — me mimicking a startled mackerel while resisting the rising urge to run away — is much the same.

Oh, she wasn't being intentionally cruel.

How was she to know about the surgeon who left me with a c-section scar and no baby to show for it. I was all fixed, goodbye, have a good life, just don't wait too long to start a family.

How was she to know about the doctor who ran the fertility tests and said everything seemed fine. But perhaps it was already too late. I found myself pulling a letter out of the mailbox with IVF stamped all over it.

And, how was she to know about the clerk who, some time later still, witnessed my signature on the papers that made it officially too late. My surname change was not, as most assume, due to marriage. The opposite, in fact.

For some, having a baby is not all rainbows and sparkles and unicorn sneezes. Trust me when I say that you're being kind by not making assumptions about this topic.

The kicker? I didn't even get a free cupcake. It's the *next* one.

I paid, picked up my box of cupcakes and booby-trapped loyalty card, and turned to leave.

I should have seen it coming. She of the glitter fingernail polish giggled. And wished me a happy Mother's Day.

At least I managed to get out of the store before the grit in my eyes and lump in my throat turned to tears.

With love,

[*illegible*]

P.S. The cupcakes were, in the end, quite delicious.

Chapter 2

Ring of Fire, A Border Realm
Oct. 30th 2012

Darling Jack and Isabella,

I have taken my own advice and made a list: Things I Cannot Live Without.

Yes, I know I should have made such a list a long time ago. And yes, I realise every single item is something my ex did not enjoy. I also realise I can't recall the last time I did most of them. But, the list is written, stuck to my fridge door next to a postcard from Juliana, and slowly, slowly, I am crossing things off.

Thus far, the entire endeavour has been a pilgrimage of sorts. I feel like I've been searching for something — except I have no idea what. Something that's been lost or dormant. Something that's just on the tip of my tongue or out of the corner of my eye.

Something that, today, I rather dramatically found.

I went hiking.

Number two on the list: get out in nature. For today's adventure, I decided on a day walk. After all, I have a good deal of time on my hands since I've been made redundant.

Ailene Cuthbertson

You would not believe how touristy the tramping tracks have gotten. Even setting out early, I left the car park with a tide of people. Trampers like me outfitted with sensible boots, packs, and all the gear, interspersed with the odd idiot flip-flopping along in jandals and jean-shorts, with tiny handbags tucked under armpits.

We streamed up the gentle gravel track in a cloud of sunscreen and chitchat. Ahead of us, over the blanket of alpine rocks and tussock, loomed the mountain.

I followed a family of four. Mum and dad strode ahead, the teenagers lagged in their wake. I couldn't help but overhear fragments of the debate — merits of a Panther versus a Tortoise — and it took me some time to figure out they were talking about tanks.

I wondered what on earth I thought I was doing. This was not the quiet day out I had in mind.

I reached the sign pointing to a short side trip to a waterfall and, in search of some sort of solitude, I changed course. Inevitably, I wasn't the only one — the armoured fighting vehicles came too.

It wasn't far.

Soon, I was following the sound of rushing water and there it was — sparkling rivulets laughing and splashing over fern-covered rocks.

I didn't realise until later exactly what I saw at the waterfall. I was about to squat at the edge of the pool when I saw that someone — a girl — had parked herself at the top of the bank. At the time, I couldn't figure out what she was doing. All I thought was, hadn't she seen the notices to stay on the track? No one else was saying anything though, and I, being the perennial non-wave-maker that I am, turned and headed back to the main track.

Ring of Fire, A Border Realm – Oct. 30th 2012

We reached the foot of the saddle and started to climb. They've made the track terribly civilised with stairs winding up the steepest gradients. I was amused to note the jandal wearers heeded the warning sign and turned back. From ahead of me, I learned far more about turret design and fields of fire than I ever wanted to know.

There's nothing quite like stairs to take a measure of how fit you are. Soon enough, my legs and lungs started to burn. I puffed and sweated and sloughed off layers of clothing. When I craned my neck to see how far I had left to go, I was barely halfway.

Why was I doing this again?

That's when I saw someone standing on the ridgeline. At least, the rock seemed to flow up and swirl around something that looked suspiciously like a figure. If it was, I have no idea how she got there. It seemed like a silly place to be taking a photo. But, no one else seemed to notice so I held my tongue.

Eventually the stairs petered out to a plateau where I joined the dotted islands of exhausted trampers, shrugged off my pack and perched on a boulder. I sat for some time, too puffed to even have a drink of water.

The view makes you feel like you're on top of the world. Spread out beneath you is a giant patchwork of hills, rivers, and lakes that roll out to a hazy horizon. A single bird, perhaps a falcon, hung in the air. I wondered what it would be like up there, flying.

When I moved on again, I was walking across a crater — a huge dust bowl scooped out of the mountain — and the stream of people spread out. At the other side, we funnelled together again at the head of the next section of track. I found it hard going. Sweat and sunscreen had already stuck my hat to my forehead and was trickling down the back of my neck. Tired muscles were indignant about having to scrabble around boulders, struggling for balance while my boots slid on the scree. And, I was becoming increasingly aware that I should've tested the tramp-worthiness of said boots with more than a stroll to the library.

I found myself behind the same family. At least by now, the talk had moved on to aircraft.

Once again, I wondered what I was doing. How's that flamin' serenity?

We reached the top. At this altitude, it was surprisingly chilly and the bitter southerly bit through my sweat-soaked shirt. I fished out my jacket and shrugged it on.

Up there, it was another world. Red earth and rocks stretched out around me and, since I was standing on an active volcano, dotted with steaming fumaroles. You'll laugh — under each one, I imagined a snorting baby dragon.

I was not the only one stopping, of course. So, in another quest for solitude, I wandered off until I was out of earshot and found a boulder to sit on.

A cup of tea heals all ills. My shoulders may not have been amused hauling a thermos up the mountain, but I certainly appreciated the cup of hot, sweet, black tea.

What I am about to tell you next requires a certain... suspension of disbelief. I remember thinking I must have been out of the wind because it got warm. Warm enough for me to take off my jacket. The air began to press into me, carrying with it the woodsy smell of a burning campfire.

It was then that I saw them — three figures wreathed in fire, their skin glowing like the embers in a blacksmith's forge. They flickered and danced and crackled towards me, ribbons of flame flying around them.

I looked wildly around but my wish for solitude had been granted.

I took a step backwards. Then another.

Some distance away, the figures halted and stared at me, coal-black eyes inscrutable.

You will think me mad. Indeed, at the time I was seriously questioning my sanity.

I was afraid. Not that they would hurt me — funnily enough, that never crossed my mind. It was the same kind of fear that has prevented me from doing a myriad of random things in the past. High school speech finals. Scooting around an ice rink on a metal frame with skate blades underneath. Trying a rock climbing wall the height of Aoraki/Mount Cook. Eating lutefisk. Going to art school. It was the stomach-knotting fear of the unknown, of failure, of being ridiculed. Accompanied by the overwhelming pull to cry off, back away, and hide under the bed.

It sounds ridiculous to me now, but I was already preparing excuses. "Sorry, creatures that can't possibly exist, but I have a headache."

Yet, I knew that if I did that, I'd walk off the mountain and return safe and sound to my mundane life, all right. But, I'd wonder — like I wondered about all the other lost opportunities — what might have been.

I moved towards them.

The prickly heat on my face and arms increased as I approached and I had to squint against the glow. One of them reached out a hand and, without thinking, I raised mine as well. As our fingers touched — theirs, unexpectedly solid — a slither of flame danced between us and licked up my arm. For one heart-stopping moment I felt scalding heat on my skin. But, they obviously had their own rules when it came to physics — the fire didn't burn. I laughed, a release of tension as much as delight, and greeted the others in the same manner.

Then, in much the same way as they'd arrived, they flickered away.

When I retrieved my pack, I sat and poured myself another cup of tea with a trembling hand.

A bray of laughter startled me. A group of trampers wandered into view, plonked themselves on boulders a stone's throw away, and pulled out sandwiches.

Time to go.

The next section of track involved sliding down volcanic rock scree, a descent which required all my concentration. I nearly came a cropper several times — my muscles were feeling strangely jelly-like.

I headed towards the famous blue and green lakes, two ancient craters filled with layers of white marl, algae, and melted snow. When I reached them, I stopped for lunch — this time welcoming the presence of people around me.

During the long walk to the bushline, I finally had time to think. For the first time since the divorce, the black hole of my future no longer seemed so empty. I could picture a path unfurling in front of me. It was not, of course, as simple as the track I followed down the mountain. In front of me, two roads diverged. Down my current route lay a continuation of my grown-up persona — responsible, fulfilling expectations, doing what I 'ought'. Or, I could go in search of magic. My magic. Because, if my encounter with the fire creatures was any indication, it's out there.

I cannot travel both.

When I read back what I've written, it seems like an obvious choice. But, you see, neither one is easy.

And, neither comes with any sort of guarantee I will find what I'm looking for. By that, of course, I'm talking about you.

As I wound my way into the bush, I stumbled across the final portent. At first, I thought someone had climbed the massive rimu and was standing on a branch. But no, only her torso had emerged from the trunk, and vines and leaves spilled from her hands.

In our youth, we'd spent enough time playing at being wood, river, and mountain nymphs to know what she was. All of them, in fact. Before me, was a dryad. The figure sitting on top of the waterfall, water flowing from her fingertips — that was a naiad. And, the one standing on the ridgeline, an oread.

I'd been surrounded by magic the whole time. But, it was like I'd had my eyes closed. I simply hadn't seen it.

I want to open my eyes.

With hope,

[*illegible*]

P.S. I shan't leave you in suspense — I know which path I shall take.

Ahead of me is a quest for magic, for my own story — and a tremendous number of things unknown. Behind me lie the tatters of what I thought I wanted, thought I *should* want, and a certain sense of failure.

I'm about to cross a threshold, and it's frightening. Oh, I shall embrace the journey, no matter where it takes me. But, I'm awfully afraid there may come a time when I'll have to let you go.

Chapter 3

West Quarter, A Bohemian Realm
May 4th 2015

Dearest Jack and Isabella,

I knew becoming an artist would be like entering another world, but little did I imagine it would be quite so literal!

I have also realised, since sending off my last letters, that the kindest thing one can say about the postal service here is: sporadic. In light of this, I feel I should set the scene before I spill the tea on my big news.

Let's start at my studio — simply because I adore it. It's a short stroll from my boarding house in the West Quarter, where us bohemians of the not-so-respectable Monde can afford. Every morning, I see Madeleine — charmingly pregnant with her second — at her pâtisserie just next door. Then, it's an expedition up five and a quarter flights of dimly-lit stairs, along a corridor that wouldn't feel out of place in a Gothic romance, and through my perpetually stuck door.

Inside, light greets me, pouring through the tall windows. It splashes onto white walls, decorative panellings, and stacks of panels, canvases, easels, and drying paintings. Along the back wall stretches a long wooden table covered in bottles, rocks, clays, plants, and instruments that look straight out of an alchemist's lab. That's where I make my pigments and paints.

I walk across a parquet floor and throw open the doors to my little balcony. All those flights of stairs are worth it — up here all I get is fresh air, a view over orange chimney pots, and the faint sounds of city-life happening on the street below.

I'm sitting at my balcony table right now. It's morning — the third moon has just faded into the pale calamine blue sky — and I am surrounded by the smell of spring, strong coffee, and freshly-baked pains au chocolat. Sparrow-like birds are hopping closer and closer, picking up my crumbs.

I am sad to think I'll be parting with all this. But, as I am also learning, one can't cross a threshold without leaving something behind.

Or perhaps, as Madeleine would say, one can't make gâteau without breaking some eggs.

Mathieu started it all. He's a painter — an exceptional one. Not that the Académie thinks so. (Oh yes, it's not just me. We've all experienced rejections from those arbiters of the fine arts.) All it took was one memorable evening, flowing with greater quantities of absinthe and frustration than usual, and the Salon du Réel was born.

The salon opened last night. I arrived at the exhibition with the thespians, invisible among their whirlwind of rouge, feathers, and daringly bare limbs. Late, of course — one can't make a sufficiently dramatic entrance without a room full of people.

Traditionally, musicians occupy this first room. Instead, installed high on a pedestal, the de Seraucourt sisters were causing quite a stir. I must have written to you about them.

West Quarter, A Bohemian Realm – May 4th 2015

You would call what they do a mélange of acrobat and contortionist. Enchanted by my tale of the fire dancers, they wore coquelicot-trimmed, skin-tight costumes that glowed like embers. Their lithe bodies entwined around each other, while ribbons of flame flew into the air. Even I, who have watched them practise many times, found it hard to tell where veils ended and illusions began.

Yes, we were being ironic when we called our salon, the Exhibition of the Real.

I slipped around the edges of the thrum. In the second room, I bumped, quite literally, into Monsieur Laurens. Me, I'd been distracted by a gentleman in the crowd spreading a truly remarkable peacock tail. And M. Laurens, he was staring at the decorative mouldings on the high ceiling.

He hasn't changed a bit since I was his student. Still the ubiquitous embroidered coats, still with tatty ends brushing the floor around his cloven hooves. Still the thick beard and thicker hair. And still no chance of confirming the rumour of a tail or horns.

I don't think I ever told you how good he was to me when I first arrived here, all wide-eyed and overwhelmed. Or how, after submitting my very first artworks for critique, his missive sat on my studio table for a week and a half before I mustered the courage to read it. It took some convincing for my stomach to ignore the pit, my fingers to unfold the paper, and my eyes to decipher his handwriting — all the while expecting the words 'useless' and 'talentless' and 'just throw it all away' to leap off the page.

Instead, I found kindness. And, under his encouraging eye, I've been able to start weaving together more and more strands of confidence.

Yes, my time here has been good for me.

"Do you see it?" he asked, gesturing ceiling-wards.

He stood in front of one of Mathieu's masterpieces, a sweeping landscape of dark mountains and stormy skies. Skies that should have contained a phoenix soaring on cadmium red wings.

I looked up. High above us, the subject of the painting was doing triumphant loop-de-loops, trailing sparks, and barely avoiding taking out the chandeliers.

I remembered very well the last time I had seen this particular artwork. Mathieu had been standing in front of it, gesturing wildly as he announced, "Our salon shall be: Of The Real." And, with a screech, the illusionary phoenix had launched itself out of the painting. (It also managed to knock over three easels, tangle itself in someone's wig, and drink a surprising amount of champagne before we corralled it in the painting again. All in all, it had been quite an evening.)

If its current antics were anything to go by, the bird had obviously enjoyed the outing.

I felt, rather than saw, the eye roll beside me.

"I suppose Mathieu's trying to make a point."

"Or thought it was funny," I replied and heard the stifled laugh as I moved on. Later on, I found out we were both correct — and I admit to being somewhat envious that I didn't think of the idea myself.

In the third room, I stopped in front of my painting.

It's very much in the style of what they teach in the ateliers here. Started with a ground of our local red-orange ochre, shapes drawn out with warm chalk and charcoal, and brought to life with textured detail in ochres, terre verte, and cerulean blue. All glazed with thin layers of transparent pigment and the lightest touch of illusion so the waterfall

West Quarter, A Bohemian Realm – May 4th 2015

splashes and laughs over the edge of the rocks. It turned out beautifully and I felt a certain satisfaction at seeing it hanging on the exhibition wall.

And, yet—

I suppose the first step is acceptance, so I shall put it in writing: lately, I seem to be suffering from a common-enough malaise around here — artist's block. I simply find it hard to sit down and paint. It's not that I don't adore putting brush to canvas, but the magic seems to have vanished. I start and stop and start again. It's taking forever to finish a piece and even then it doesn't feel... right.

Here's what I have discovered.

Being an artist isn't about the pencil stub tangled in your messy up-do, the battered sketchbook jammed into your back pocket, or the paint-splattered shirt barely covering your tortured soul. It's not all listening to colours, sighing words like 'juxtapose' or 'ephemeral', or having 3,318 mood swings by morning tea. Rather, it's about continually answering the question, why bother?

Why bother stepping through the studio door when you don't have the time and you're just too tired. There's that mountain of dishes waiting in the kitchen, Madeleine's birthday present to run out and collect, and the builder to meet about fixing that wall. Maybe, just maybe, you can find sixteen seconds to have a nap because there's a humdinger of a headache creeping up behind your eyeballs — and it's putting on its boxing gloves. Tomorrow, you tell yourself, I'll try tomorrow.

Why bother facing the blank canvas anyway — it never turns out like you imagined. It's supposed to be in your 'style' (although, you're probably the only artist in the worlds without one). It's supposed to be finely detailed with a certain textured rawness. It's supposed to be calm and filled with tempestuous emotion. It's supposed to be a thing of beauty while also revealing a hidden truth about the worlds. And, most importantly, it's supposed to be absolutely, utterly *original*. At least there's the dishes to scrub while waiting for your muse to drop by.

Why bother putting your art into the world — no one really cares. Florentine from downstairs sells out a collection in three and a half minutes, and you? All of your paintings end up sitting in your studio collecting dust. Wait, I exaggerate — sometimes people do take notice. Exhibition-goers raise an eyebrow and point a finger at the price tag beside your painting — as though what it took to walk into the studio and go from blank canvas to laying down every single brushstroke isn't *worth* anything. Critics happily tell you of their desire to rip the dragon hatchling out of your painting, hurl it to the floor, and stomp on its head. You would be right in thinking that, frankly, having no one care is preferable.

But *you* care. That's why you bother. That's what makes you step through the studio door, face the blank canvas, put your art into the world. That's what calls you to create, why you're an artist.

Oh, the actual reason changes all the time. It has to. You can't stay the same forever, after all. But this is life and it's a messy sort of endeavour. More often than not, there's an intermission in between losing the way and finding a new story to believe in.

That's where I am, it seems — waiting in the wings and searching for what's calling me next.

All of which goes a fair way towards explaining my big news. The whole objective of this letter was to tell you

West Quarter, A Bohemian Realm – May 4th 2015

about Lady Clement. Yes, *the* Lady Cecille Clement — worlds-famous adventuress, explorer, naturalist, archaeologist, and goodness knows besides.

I confess, I did not recognise her when she stepped up beside me. I did think her bobbed hair, smart culottes, and precisely knotted cravat delightfully scandalous, even for the West Quarter.

Once she ascertained I was the artist of the painting, she turned startling violet eyes on me and asked, "And this is your reality? Naiads on top of waterfalls?"

When I agreed, she gave a brisk nod.

"Good", she said, "I invite you to join my expedition."

It turns out she has discovered a lost city — or perhaps more accurately, a lost valley full of ancient ruins — and, "I require an artist to document the ghosts."

She reminded me of my cousin, Juliana. You remember Juliana? Infectious laugh. Animals adore her. We can talk until the end of time without running out of things to say. The best person to have adventures with.

It was then that I made up my mind — I just didn't know it yet.

Later in the evening, when my judgemental inner voices emerged — informing me that I didn't have the skill, I was too old, and I certainly couldn't afford the trip — I strode up to Lady Clement and told her, "Yes."

I leave in what you would call a week.

I've always wanted to be an adventuress and explorer. Just imagine, we may discover dragons!

With love and mille bisous,

[*illegible*]

P.S. I found a family here and I will be sad to say goodbye.

It feels awfully like the first time I was made redundant. It wasn't so much the closing of the entire office or losing our jobs — but when our close-knit team scattered, the camaraderie and solidarity got lost as well.

I hope Lady Clement's team is welcoming.

Chapter 4

---

*An Island Off The Edge Of The Map,
An Undisclosed Realm
Jan. 16th 2016*

My dear Jack and Isabella,

You find me with too much to tell you!

You will be eager, I know, to hear more about my archaeological escapades. My previous letters, they barely scratch the surface of the layers upon layers of ghosts and memories among the ruins.

But, that shall have to wait. Because today was the most marvellous day any human has ever had, in the history of humankind (or at least since they got the printing press up and running).

You'd go straight past the entrance unless you knew it was there. Even Nereida, the team's naturalist, remains tight-lipped about how she discovered it.

As you enter the small bay, all you see is a curve of ultra-marine blue water meeting a shoreline of sun-bleached rocks, driftwood, and bush-covered hills. Today, there wasn't a cloud in the sky. It stretched over us, the same colour as the sea.

We edged the boat — with its surprisingly modern outboard — closer to the shore until we could see the gap and ribbon of water behind it. Slowly, we slipped around boulders lurking just under the waves, past steep banks of rock, and into the cove. Blue-green water stretched out in a rippling sheet, shaded darker at the edges by trees, and brightened in the middle by the reflection of the sky.

I was leaning over the side of the boat, keeping watch for submerged boulders, when one of the shadows moved. I may have yelped in surprise. Nereida laughed at me.

As our boat slid on through the water, I saw more and more movement. Slick bodies darted under the boat and flashed away. They appeared quite human, save for long, diaphanous fins that cascaded down their lower limbs.

The locals, Nereida told me, call them water dancers. Elsewhere, they have other names: mermaids, nymphs, sea sprites, or even sirens.

Yes, it astonished me as well. My companion, on the other hand — turns out she's something of a specialist in mythological aquatic creatures.

She was there to catalogue the clans. The cove, I learned, is a nursery — mermaids migrate tremendous distances to return there. Each clan has their own distinctive colouring and fin shapes. After a while, I began to see what Nereida meant and started to point out a streak of scarlet or ruffles. She took notes in her journal.

At the edges of the largest pool, we found the mermaid adults lounging on the sun-soaked rocks. No one took much notice of us. No one moved much either, save for the occasional ponderous roll. Gangs of pups, though, more than made up for their elders' lethargy. They roared between the rocks and water, singing with excited whistles and clacks. Apparently there's a technical term, but Nereida calls it their 'play song'. I have to mention it, because it was quite pervasive (and this idyllic scene is in need of a spot of realism): the air smelled distinctly of fish.

Nereida was consulting her notes with a frown. "Do you remember seeing a dark blue body with yellow double caudal fins?"

I had not. That was a problem — all the clans should have arrived at the cove by now.

Nereida might be a naturalist and a scientist but she clearly cares about her charges. She checked our fuel level and re-checked the weather report. The next faring light, she says, is fairly close. We'll go see if we can find them.

We turned, I waved goodbye to the little ones (who were too busy to wave back), and we slid out of the cove. Pointing the bow towards the open sea, Nereida opened the throttle.

Engine roaring, the boat skimmed over the light chop, flinging wind in our faces and spray in our wake. It didn't take long to get there. Soon, I was pointing out a quiet glow beneath the waves. We slowed. That, it seemed, was the faring light.

Next time I'm sailing, I shall have to keep an eye out. Faring lights are not all that uncommon — there are strings of them all over the oceans to guide mermaids on their migratory paths. They're just easily mistaken for bioluminescent plankton.

I saw the dorsal fin first, then a sleek blue-black body torpedoed through the water. By the time Nereida had turned her head, there were more. Dolphins surrounded the boat, snorting clouds of water. In unison, a duo whooshed out of the waves, slapping their tails with a crack as they fell back in. Farther out, another leaped, somersaulted, and disappeared into the water with an even louder smack.

We couldn't help but laugh in delight. And then, as if by magic, the mermaids appeared. Larger blue-black bodies rolled lazily under the boat, trailing gossamer yellow fins and luminescence — the clan we were looking for.

Nereida cut the engine. We bobbed happily, listening to the tink of the waves against the hull, the dolphins' puffing snorts, and a low hum coming from the mermaids. There is a technical term, of course, but Nereida calls it their 'inviting song'.

"Let's join them," she said. We stripped down to our wetsuits and slid over the side of the boat. Cold water closed over my head. I came up gasping, only to meet a salty splash to the face.

"It was a dolphin," Nereida called.

No, I can't say I believed her either.

There's something about things rising from unknown watery depths that speaks to a rather primal fear. Of course I knew exactly who was in the water with us, but that didn't stop my shriek. All of a sudden, I was tossed into the air, before hitting the swelling wave with a fountainous splash and a tangle of windmilling limbs.

Once again, I surfaced, trying to inhale more air than water and scrape hair out of my eyes. I heard Nereida laughing.

"Like this," she sang out, and proceeded to demonstrate an elegant tuck, arms hugging her knees to her chest before making a splashy landing. If memory serves, I think you'd call it a cannonball.

If you'd told me that, one day, I would be having a noisy water fight with dolphins and mermaids, I'd have said you were nuts. I can't say I really got the hang of it. But it didn't matter because, oh boy, was it the most fun I've ever had.

Off the Edge of the Map, An Undisclosed Realm – Jan. 16th 2016

And, for the first time in what seems like forever, I found myself letting go. Really, truly letting go. Completely forgetting to worry about being gangly, uncoordinated, looking stupid, or doing the wrong thing. Instead, laughing so much my belly hurt, the whole of my existence dedicated entirely to splashing water.

I'm not entirely sure who won but it was not us humans. Although, for clumsy, land-born creatures, I believe we acquitted ourselves rather well. Our downfall was the gales of laughter — a natural reaction, but one that inevitably led to us swallowing our body weights in sea water.

Eventually, Nereida and I hauled our soggy selves back into the boat and collapsed, giggling and gasping.

That, I found out, was why the mermaid clan hadn't yet made it to the cove: they were mucking about in the water having a good time with the dolphins.

I think they've got the right idea. Too often, we think we need to hurtle along at ludicrous speed to get where we want to go. It's all about reaching the destination, no time for anything that happens along the way. But all those missed experiences add up to an awful lot of missed magic. Instead, when taking time to treat the journey like a series of grand adventures, a funny thing happens: we attain something far more valuable than a mere goal — we get stories.

Stories like this one.

Always remember to stop and play with the dolphins.

With love and splashes,

[illegible]

Chapter 5

The Nest, An Island Realm
Feb. 14th 2018

Darling Jack and Isabella,

This morning was the perfect morning for flying.

I suppose I must mention — in case my last letter has not yet reached you — that no, of course mermaids don't fly! I left their clan some time ago. You'll be astonished to hear what I'm doing now — something that has always been a particular dream of mine.

Let me introduce you to Imperious — magnificent creature that she is. She is intelligent and beautiful and truly worthy of her name. Also, she is beside me as I write. I believe dragons possess a good deal more intelligence than most people credit them with.

Imperious and I have no shortage of escapades we could regale you with. But, in the end, I've decided to take a cue from the dragonish life-in-the-moment attitude and tell you about our perfectly ordinary flight today.

This morning, Imperious was of the opinion it was the perfect morning for sunning herself. She lay — or perhaps more accurately, lolled — across her rock. As my boots crunched over the grit towards her, she cracked open one iridescent eye, took in the harness and mail pouch slung over my shoulder, and promptly slid her eye closed.

There's a reason I call her Imp.

Even early in the morning, it's hot up there on the plateau. The sort of hot that makes your face permanently glisten, your clothes stick to your body, and wearing riding leathers highly uncomfortable. Mercifully, I seem to have cultivated some sort of heat immunity since the fire dancers. Even so, it's a relief to get flying and into the cool air.

The dragons usually have other ideas.

If you've never had to move a recalcitrant horned dragon before, here's a tip: loquats. It's no coincidence the island is covered in orchards, let me tell you!

I presented Imp with her treats. She sighed, raised her magnificent head, and regarded me thoughtfully. I waited. Dealing with dragons has taught me a good deal of patience. Eventually, she huffed, hauled her belly off her rock, and stretched like a cat. Muscles rippled from head to tail, and back again, finishing in a fang-filled yawn. And, as usual, she expressed her displeasure at having to move by taking her time sliding down the ridge, pebbles and sand scattering and clattering around her.

I've learned that dragons are naturally dominant and Imp is a prime example. So I was ready to block her large, scaled nose as it swung towards me. It stopped just shy of butting my pocket.

Have I mentioned there's a reason I call her Imp?

After her huge jaws snapped up the loquats, she honoured me by lowering her head so I could scratch her eye ridges. You know you've got the correct spot when her lower lip starts to quiver. It's cute. And by 'cute', of course I mean, resplendent.

The Nest, An Island Realm – Feb. 14th 2018

Imp is trained to her harness in much the same way as equestrians tack up their horses back home. I admit, I disregarded a few centuries of tradition in doing so. But, funnily enough, now some of the other riders are copying the approach — even my most vocal critic.

First, Imp pokes her nose through the headband of the halter and I flick the strap over the crest of her head and tie it. Then, she crouches so I can slide the harness over her shoulders and buckle it under her. Finally, with a tap on her foreleg, she swings her huge nose under my shin to give me a boost up.

This morning, as I settled in the saddle, tightening buckles and strapping on my mail pouch, I felt Imp start to tremble beneath me. With her quietly lashing tail and eyes on the sky, I knew exactly what she had in mind. And, while exhilarating, a vertical leap into the air followed by swooping loops and victory rolls is not the most peaceful way to spend a flight.

Some of my happiest childhood memories are riding the horses through the farm paddocks with my cousin, Juliana. You remember Juliana? Infectious grin. Writes detailed lists for everything from shopping, to a trip away, to books to read. Has a knack for making everyone around her comfortable. Horse-mad and extremely good at it.

Unlike my cousin, I could never claim to be anything more than a passable equestrienne. However, some of the skills I absorbed from her have certainly come in handy when it comes to training dragons.

Especially ones who live up to the name of Imp.

Crouched atop Imp's shoulders, I nudged her and requested a calm pirouette. Emphasis on *calm*. She grumbled. And went round on her haunches in a spin worthy of a battle-trained dragon. Fortunately, this morning she didn't turf me to the dust — a not-so-graceful move I have often practised in the past. (They make a balm for sore muscles and bruises here that's akin to arnica and I used to practically bathe in the stuff.)

For some time, we continued to dance, kicking up a small sandstorm. Just a normal part of our pre-flight checks. Finally, with a huff, she settled and decided to start listening to her rider.

Being one of the dominant dragons (as I'm sure you can tell), Imperious holds a ridge near the takeoff drop. As we shambled over, I pulled my scarf over my mouth and nose and snapped on my goggles.

I do hope you get the chance to go horse riding one day. But I'm afraid it's nothing like riding a dragon. Flying is pure freedom and flying with Imp — glorious.

I felt her huge muscles bunch under me. At my signal, with a lunge and spray of grit, we fell off the cliff. It's like screaming down a zip-line — without the line. Imp was feeling nice. She didn't leave it to the last second to snap out her wings and claw the air, and our plummet stalled in a heady rush of wind.

The dragons live in what translates as the Nest — a large, flat crater on a still-steaming volcano ringed by mountains. As you glide away, forest-covered peaks roll beneath you. The peaks turn into grassy hills. Then the hills flatten out into a low-lying river valley carved into fields and dotted with settlements.

This morning, Imp magnanimously ignored the small, crunchy sheep. She sometimes doesn't.

When we reached tussock, sand, and foaming waves, we banked to head east into the sun. Bright rays slid over Imp's head and glinted all the way across outstretched wings. Even with my goggles, I had to squint into the light. It wouldn't worry Imp. Dragons have sets of transparent membranes that slide protectively over their eyes for precisely these sorts of conditions.

It doesn't take long before the coastline ends, and then we're soaring over the archipelago — my favourite place to fly. Oh, you should have seen it this morning. Ahead of us, mountains faded blue and purple into the morning haze. Beneath us, tree-green islands and peninsulas curved around flat stretches of turquoise sea. And, scattered throughout, the occasional pool of woolly, white clouds.

Remind me to tell you about the sport they play here — it's a local obsession. The closest I can come is polo, except that polo ponies don't use low-lying clouds as cover.

Nearer the strait — the channel of water between the main islands — we started to find clumps of low, dark clouds. Imp grunted in agreement as I leaned to the side and we banked to glide around them. Flying in the rain is not our idea of fun.

Entering the strait itself though, we didn't have much choice. A low blanket of grey cloud lay over the white-tipped sea. And, as is often the case, it was raining.

Imp twisted uncomfortably as the first drops hit her scales. Even in my flying leathers, scarf, and goggles, I could feel the pinprick stings. And the water slashing my eyes made it rather hard to see. Imp has that protective membrane over her eyes, so I hunkered down, hid my face, and trusted the dragon to fly us through.

I won't bore you with the details of this passage. It takes about what you would call an hour. An hour of the steady whoosh of dragon wings, the occasional stomach-heaving drop as we hit a pocket of unexpected air, the cold gradually seeping into your body.

There are mountains on both sides of the strait which means the whole thing forms a natural wind funnel. And, if you thought the ride had been a rollercoaster thus far, just wait until you fly out of the rain and can see the hills on the other side.

Without needing to be told, Imp veered to follow the coastline. I stayed glued to her back and the crosswinds buffeted and jolted us along.

Dragons land with the aerodynamism of a bowl of petunias. So you'll understand when I tell you that the landing strips — essentially long swimming pools — are a centuries-old tradition I'm perfectly happy with.

Imp pointed her nose inland and began our descent. We swooped lower over the bay's only island, over the white sails of small boats, and over the foaming waves. At what always seems like the last second, with a great hauling back and flapping of wings, we hit the water. As the rider, you're only vaguely aware of the walls of foam that rise on both sides of you. What takes over your senses is the crescendo of noise. It's like a drum kit crashing down stairs. Or the shattering of eight thousand stained-glass windows — onto the drum kit.

Imp was still feeling nice. I sat up in the harness and pulled off my goggles and scarf with not a drop of water on me. Some dragons take it as a point of pride to never get their riders wet. Imp uses it to let me know her mood.

Unlike finned dragons, horned dragons do not enjoy being wet. It never takes much to coax Imp onto the bank. She shook herself like a cat — delicately flicking water droplets off one outstretched front foot, and then the other.

The Nest, An Island Realm – Feb. 14th 2018

Of course, in the direction of the postmaster who was waiting for us. With a dragon like Imp, he and I often find ourselves at odds. But, behind that scowl and beard of Dwarven bushiness, I think he has a soft spot for my dragon. True to form, he offered Imp loquat treats before reaching up to take my mail pouch.

The settlement on this island is far larger than our own. Next to the dragons' landing area is the port, then the commercial quarter, and then houses all through the steep bush-covered hills. Right at the summit is an area much like our Nest, where Imp also has a rock she calls home.

First though, I needed to care for my mount. I pointed Imp towards the large sandy arena next to the landing strips, unbuckling and untying myself from the harness as we ambled over. Once there, I tapped her shoulder and she crouched so I could slide down.

I remember dismounting after my first long flight. The moment my boots hit the ground, my legs gave way like jelly and I fell on my derrière in an embarrassing puddle. Happily, I've gained some muscles since then!

Imp and I made quick work of removing her harness and I knew her well enough to step hurriedly away. She lost no time in flopping onto her back, wiggling in the sand in a most undignified manner. And by 'undignified', of course I mean, impressive.

A groom appeared, handed me Imp's after-flight kit, grinned at the cheerfully flailing dragon, and left us to it. I've never understood why some riders think they're above rubbing down their dragons. It's one of my favourite times — especially with a glorious creature like Imperious.

While I waited for Imp to finish her roll, I rummaged through the kit for the cloth we use to polish dragon scales.

It's soft and prepared in a sort of oil that smells not entirely unlike lavender.

Here's another surprising thing I have learned about dragons — they purr. Every time, as soon as I start to rub down Imp, a low rumble emanates from deep in her chest. It's loud! Which makes sense — after all, she is much, much larger than a cat.

And, this is where you find me as I write this letter. I sit with the sun warming my face, a still-purring, lavender scented dragon against my back, and paper resting on one leather-clad knee.

Soon, I'll head to the barracks to clean Imp's harness and then join the other riders for lunch. Imp will do her vertical takeoff and fly to the summit with a trumpeting cry. I used to think she was greeting the other dragons. Now, I think it's more likely she's warning them to get off her rock.

I shall give this letter to the postmaster but I have no expectation of it reaching you any time soon. How ironic to have postal dragons at my disposal, yet still have no way to send correspondence reliably. I suppose that's what I get for being so far out in the wop-wops. But, I have to tell you — I love it here. I do wish you were here to share it with me.

With love,

[*illegible*]

P.S. I didn't want to write this. But you must be wondering what happened to little Luna — the orphan hatchling who was foisted on me when I first arrived.

There is no good way to say this: she died. She went down quite suddenly. And, before I realised just how seriously ill she was, she was dying in my arms. I doubt she knew I was there at the end — but it comforts me to believe she did.

Dragons don't mourn their own but I have more than made up for it. I'm afraid I cannot even write this without crying so please forgive the ink smudges.

As much as everyone assures me she lived a good life, I did everything I could, and dragons aren't as hardy as they look — it does not help.

I miss her. I miss her chirpy greetings, how she raced up to see me, the little black nose that pushed its way into everything I was doing. I miss how she'd press into me for hugs when I knelt down, how she'd mosey quietly along in my wake as I went about my chores, how she'd sit on my lap and burp.

Everywhere I go, there are reminders of her and the things she did. For the longest time, I worried about her, especially when the weather was cold and wet.

I wish she'd had more time. She was barely a year old.

I feel like I failed her. As you can imagine, my old nemesis came roaring back. After all, this is simply more proof I would have made a terrible mother, so it's a good thing I never had children.

Don't worry.

I think I'll take a leaf out of Imp's book and tell that perennially muckraking nemesis to get off my rock.

Chapter 6

Waikato, New Zealand
May 8th 2022

Dear Jack and Isabella,

If I summed up my afternoon in one word, it would have to be: damp.

How quickly one acclimatises to the desert — although I still suspect the fire dancers had something to do with my heat tolerance. I woke this morning to ringing bells, while grey sand and sky melted into gold. By the time I entered the brouhaha of the markets in search of breakfast, the cool dawn breeze had been replaced by shimmering heat. Imp, of course, didn't mind. Also, being a mythical winged saurian, she was thoroughly spoiled there.

Yes, the lamplight, music, smoke, and fortune tellers' carpets of the night markets seem a long way away now. Picture me at a park picnic table — sitting on my jacket because the seat is wet — under an overcast sky and a tree that insists on periodically shaking water and gold-tinged leaves onto me. If I were anywhere else in the worlds, I would expect to hear the dryad snickering.

I have, on the table in front of me, a sparkly, rainbow-coloured cupcake (I can tell you with the benefit of personal experience it looks *nothing* like a unicorn sneeze). It made me think of you.

It feels like a dozen lifetimes have passed since I last wandered into that shop but, funnily enough, it hasn't changed much. Same quasi-Victorian tea room vibe, same sweet treats, same pink uniform behind the counter.

At least I finally got the free cupcake!

I seem to recall that's when I started writing to you, that last visit. Goodness knows why. I remember hazy thoughts of jotting down some of the things I wish I could've told you. Maybe this is a way I can leave something of value in the worlds, a legacy of sorts. More likely, I simply wrote these letters to get the thoughts out of my head. Because, if truth be told, I have written things in these letters I cannot say out loud.

Whatever the reason, what has emerged is something entirely different — a story. My story. A tale not unlike this cupcake — layers of tumultuous, rich, red velvet adorned with rainbow frosting and magical sparkles.

Life isn't linear — it's a process of becoming. We spiral between starting and stopping and starting again. We change direction, let go of dreams, pick up new ones. But, along the way, we get better at knowing it's the journey that matters, not the destination. We get better at rediscovering ourselves whenever we get lost. We get better at going and growing out on a limb, following our noses, our inklings, our inner voice that says, "yes!" And, most of all, we get better at opening our eyes and seeing the magic.

Yes, here I am, turning my life into my own story and I adore it. Instead of letting life just happen to me, I'm something that happens to life!

Waikato, New Zealand – May 8th 2022

I'm just sorry that having children — having you — is one of the dreams I had to let go.

So, this will be my last letter but certainly not my last adventure. I leave this evening to meet my cousin, Juliana. We have decided to run away and join the circus.

Adieu my darlings.

[*illegible*]

P.S. My next letter will be addressed to the inland revenue department. It is a grave oversight that there are no tax codes for bohemian artist, ghost archaeologist, airship engineer, mermaid naturalist, dragon rider, and goodness knows besides.

P.P.S. The tree did have a dryad! I shared my cupcake with her. The sparkles made her sneeze.

Acknowledgements

I've always wanted to write a book. And I couldn't have done it without these amazing people.

Thank you to Blobbs "have you seen my tractor key" for your love and support, always bringing a thermos of tea on our adventures, and all the excessively detailed feedback that made this book so much better.

Thank you to Marie "it's a two tea morning" for all the holidays, the most epic campervan trip ever, and excellent suggestions when I couldn't think of the words.

Thank you to Flavia "I painted" for the chats, support, and delightful feedback on a very rough first draft.

Thank you to Aimee "I do a good line in copy editing" for the encouragement and rounding up those pesky missing hyphens.

Thank you to Vicky Quinn Fraser "it doesn't have to be 80,000 words of a Very Serious Book, instead write a Micro Book", author, book coach, and founder of Moxie Books, for helping me make this book a reality.

And lastly, thank you to all the animals — the horses, cows, sheep, chickens, ducks, dogs, cats, and particularly certain rapscallion just-eating-your-gumboots goats — who make up Imp.

About the Author

Ailene Cuthbertson is an artist, creative writer, creativity coach, and advocate for connecting with your magic and living your own Tale Of Me: A Collection of Good Bits.

As a teenager, she spent a lot of time in libraries escaping into all the books. This meant she could fill her high-school English teachers' lives with joy. She followed instructions to 'write what you know' precisely — with stories of swashbuckling pirates, mysterious wanderers, and one memorable ambassador doing a really bad job on a far-flung star. It goes without saying that every heroine bore a suspicious resemblance to her. She also produced fantastic research projects — especially that one year she decided the whole thing was boring and invented an archaeological dig site. The ghosts, she discovered later on.

Fast forward a few years and she figured she'd better grow up and get on with being a mundane, non-magical human. That didn't go terribly well. So, she's not doing that anymore.

Now, when not creating stories full of magic and wonder, you'll find her following faring lights, crossing the wall, storming the castle, or working as a software developer because she also loves being a nerd.

Find Ailene and her art online at oldmountainart.com and her creativity coaching at flowontheroad.com.

www.ingramcontent.com/pod-product-compliance
Lightning Source LLC
Chambersburg PA
CBHW032018290426
44109CB00013B/710